Look Out, Nebit!

Written by Katie Dale

Illustrated by Aleksandar Zolotić

Collins

My little dog Nebit is my best friend.

We stay close to each other ...

most of the time.

"Oh no! Look out, Nebit!"

3

Nebit runs across the crowded street.

The muck spreaders are smearing stinky dung around the houses to keep the rats away.

But where is little Nebit?

Oh no! He's kicked over the mucky bucket.

"Look out, Nebit!"

Oh no! Nebit scurries into a rich house.

The cook is roasting antelope for dinner.

Look out, Nebit!

Nebit scuttles into the bathroom.

How odd! A lady is filling a pool with milk to make her skin soft.

But where is little Nebit?

Splash!

Oh no! He's spilt all the milk.

"Look out, Nebit!"

Don't cry over spilt milk!

Nebit sprints to the river.

Fishermen are looking for fish for their dinner.

But where is little Nebit?

Oh no! The fisherman is angry. He has lost all his fish.

"Look out, Nebit!"

Nebit bounds on to the boats.

One boat is even decorated with flowers – maybe the queen is inside!

But where is little Nebit?

Oh no! He's pushed the girl's ladder.

"Look out, Nebit!"

Nebit leaps over the stepping stones ...

But help! These are not stones!

Snap!

15

Nebit escapes into the desert.

The giant sphinx stares down at me.

But where is little Nebit?

Oh no! Don't wake the grumpy camels.

"Look out, Nebit!"

Spit!

Nebit disappears down a shadowy tunnel.

There are drawings that tell a story.

Nebit?

But where is Nebit?

How will I find him in the dark?

Is he lost forever?

Suddenly I *smell* him!

"There you are, my stinky little Nebit. Hurray!
Let's go home – and I'll hold your lead tight
this time!"

Woof!

Finding Nebit

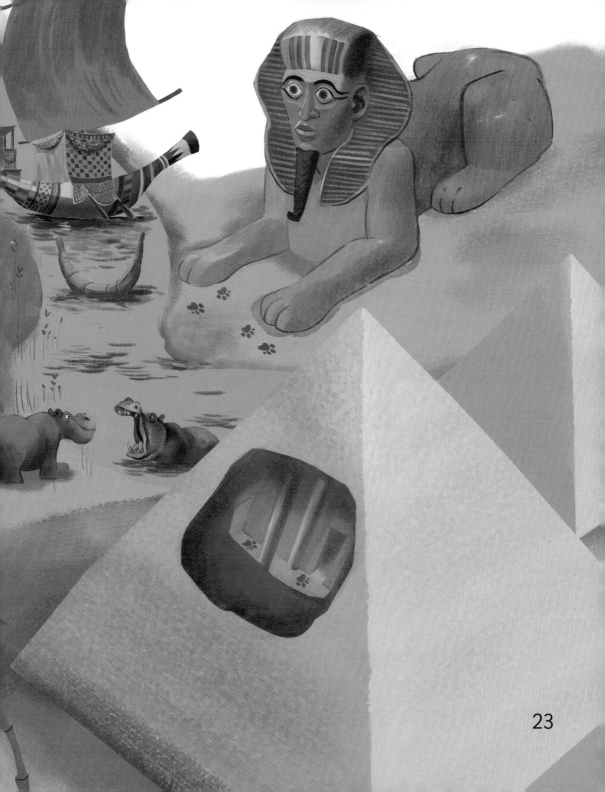

 Review: After reading

Use your assessment from hearing the children read to choose any GPCs, words or tricky words that need additional practice.

Read 1: Decoding

- Talk about how the same sound can be written in different ways. For example, the /f/ sound in the following words:

  flowers   fish   sphinx

- Ask the children to sound out and blend each word:

  f/l/ow/er/s   f/i/sh   s/ph/i/n/x

- Talk about the different ways that the /f/ sound is spelled in these words.
- Can the children think of any other words that contain the /f/ sound spelled "ph"? (e.g. *phone, photo, elephant*)

Read 2: Prosody

- Choose two double page spreads and model reading with expression to the children. Ask the children to have a go at reading the same pages with expression.
- Show the children how you pause for ellipses to build tension.
- Reread the whole book to model fluency and rhythm in the story.

Read 3: Comprehension

- For every question ask the children how they know the answer. Ask the children:
  - Why do you think the boy says that he and Nebit stay close to each other **most of the time** at the start of the story?
  - Why was the fisherman **angry**? (*Nebit made him drop his fish*)
  - Why did the boy put a lead on Nebit at the end of the story?
  - How do you think the boy felt when he walked into the tunnel on page 18?
  - What was your favourite part of this story? Why?